OUR ANIMAL FRIENDS

THE HERMIT CRAB

KATESALIN PAGKAIHANG

About the Author

I love all kinds of animals, and
photography is my greatest passion.

Every time I am on a tropical beach,
my eyes search for tiny hermit crabs.
I like watching them live freely in nature,
greeting one another when they meet.
I try to stay still, but if they see my slight
movements, they quickly hide inside their
shells. After a while, they peek out to see
if it is safe to come out again. I also enjoy
walking along the beach at night, especially
when the moon is full. Hundreds of hermit
crabs come out to socialize.

Books have opened many doors for me.
I hope this photo book will introduce young
readers to the natural world. I believe
nature is the best home for animals.

Save nature! Save wildlife!

To everyone who respects Mother Nature.

Hello, friend!
We are hermit crabs—crustaceans just like lobsters, shrimp, crayfish, or crabs. We have ten legs, the first of which are claws. The left claw is larger than the right and hard, and it has a large pincher at the end that covers the entrance to the shell. It is also our weapon. Our next two pairs of legs are for walking, and we use the two smallest pairs to hold onto our shell.

Hermit crabs have two movable stalks with eyes on top.
Our eyes are highly sensitive to the movement around us.
This helps us protect ourselves from predators.

We have two pairs of antennae that help us touch, feel, taste, and smell the world around us.

6

There are more than 1,000 species of hermit crabs
all over the world. They are divided into two groups: marine
and land hermit crabs.

Marine hermit crabs live in saltwater, hiding around coral.
Some of us have other living things growing on our shell.
These creatures help us by stinging our predators,
and we help them by giving them our leftovers to eat.

Land hermit crabs live most of our life on land. Some species require access to both freshwater and saltwater. We also need high humidity in the air to survive. We cannot breathe underwater.

Hermit crabs are brown, gray, red,
or orange, depending on the species.
Our average lifespan is 15–30 years.
Some land hermit crabs can live as long as 50 years.

Hermit crabs are sociable creatures. We need lots of friends. We live in large colonies of 100 or more. It is easy to change shells or find food when we have lots of friends around.

14

We are nocturnal animals, which means we are active during the night. After sunset we walk around. We love climbing, digging, looking for food, and eating. We eat everything! We love fruits, meat, seaweed, insects, leaves, and bark.

We can be as tiny as 1 centimeter
or as big as 40 centimeters long, depending on our species.

One female hermit crab carries hundreds of eggs. She lays the eggs and holds them inside her shell until it is time for them to hatch in the ocean.

After we hatch from our eggs, young land hermit crabs need to find suitable shells before we leave the ocean to start our life on land.

Hermit crabs cannot produce shells. We have soft abdomens, so we use abandoned shells from sea snails to protect us and to be our mobile homes. We choose shells that have washed onto the beach based on their shape, size, weight, and space. A new shell has to fit our body.

Our shell collects water in it,
keeping us wet. This is good for our sensitive body,
as we need lots of humidity in order to breathe.

Without a shell, we cannot survive.

We shed our old skin when we grow new skin. This process is called molting. We dig in the sand and bury ourselves while we molt. The sand keeps us warm, wet, and safe from enemies. Adult hermit crabs molt once every 18 months, and young hermit crabs molt every few months. After molting, our bodies grow, and it is time to move on to a bigger shell.

A broken shell is better than no shell!
But a broken shell lets our body dry out faster, and we cannot protect ourselves from predators like seagulls, larger crabs, sharks, sea stars, squids, or octopuses.

"Uh oh! I can't fit my legs in. I need a better shell."

In order to look for a new home,
we check out one another's shells when we meet to see
if any might be the right size for a shell exchange.

If we find an abandoned shell that is too big for us, we might wait for another hermit crab to come. When the new hermit crab shows up, we inspect the shell to see if it fits the new hermit crab. If it is still too big, we wait together. Sometimes we get a big group of hermit crabs. We form a line from largest to smallest and exchange shells by moving up to the next shell in line. The biggest hermit crab in the group moves into the abandoned shell we have discovered. The process may take many hours of waiting, but it is worth the wait if everyone gets a bigger, better home.

Shells are beautiful.
They come in a variety of shapes and colors.

Some people collect shells, making it difficult for us to find a new home when our body gets bigger and cannot fit in our old, small shell anymore.

We often walk around looking for a bigger shell here and there.

Many hermit crabs use trash as our mobile homes.
But it is hard for us to fit into the pieces of trash we find.
They are surely not a good home for us!

When there are not many shells around, other hermit crabs might try to take our shell, leading to a fight. If we do not feel like fighting, we can avoid the fight by covering ourselves . . .

"Nope!"

"Would you like to exchange shells?"

until they leave us alone.

"Okie dokie! Don't worry. I'll go find somewhere else."

Otherwise, hermit crabs have a simple life.

We are wild animals, and nature is our home.

There is lots to do, like hanging out with friends…

and exploring nature.

We enjoy long walks on the beach.

"Whoops! I didn't see that coming."

If the sun gets too hot, we just find a good place to rest...

and, of course, take a nap.

We also like to play hide-and-seek.

"Nature is beautiful, and life is full of joy."

Copyright © 2017 by Katesalin Pagkaihang

All Rights Reserved. No part of this publication may be reproduced, distributed, or transmitted in any form or by any means, including photocopying, recording, or other electronic or mechanical methods, without the prior written permission of the publisher, except in the case of brief quotations embodied in critical reviews and certain other noncommercial uses permitted by copyright law.

All photos were either taken by the author (Katesalin Pagkaihang).

Printed in the United States of America
First Printing 2017
ISBN (Paperback) 978-616-445-039-4
Published by Katesalin Pagkaihang
www.katesalinpagkaihang.com

Additional resources
Uniserv.BUU
Peta.org